Two Little Witchlings series

Ostara:
The Hare & the Kingfisher

Written & Illustrated by
Becky Susan Adams

"Dedicated to my wonderful readers.
Thank you for your brilliant support!"

Spring Equinox was around the corner, and Rose Witchling & Lily Witchling were out collecting sweet treats for the Festival of Trees. As luck would have it, they had managed to find a large patch of wild strawberries!

"Just as they started home, Lily Witchling spotted something small & colourful lying on a rock. It was a little Kingfisher, cold & frail, and it looked very sick.

"What happened to it?" asked Rose Witchling with a furrowed brow.

"I'm not sure," replied her Big Sister. "Let's take it home to Mama, she will know what to do."

Mama decided that the best thing would be to give the tiny bird a dose of chamomile tea to help it sleep, then snuggle it in a blanket next to the fireplace. She put two bowls of milk & honey next to it just in case it awoke hungry or thirsty in the night.

"We've done all we can, my loves," she said to her daughters. "Whatever happens next, it's in the hands of the Goddess. Come on, let's get some sleep, and check on our new friend in the morning."

But when the sun came up, they couldn't find their little houseguest anywhere. Mama checked the kitchen. Lily Witchling checked the garden. Rose Witchling was just checking the pantry, and jumped in surprise when out came a Huge Hare with an armful of carrots!

"I'm so sorry, I didn't mean to startle you," explained the Hare. "I was just really hungry, and I've already eaten all the milk & honey."

"Who are you?" asked Rose Witchling.

"I am the Kingfisher you found," replied the Hare. "Or, at least, I was. Ostara the Goddess changed me. It's a long story."

"I'd love to hear it!" Rose Witchling responded. "We all would!"

"So she led the Big Bunny to Mama & Lily Witchling, and after explaining who he was to her bewildered family, he told them what happened.

"You see, every year the divine maiden Ostara waits for Winter's grip to loosen, and then she swoops in and brings Springtime. But this year, Ostara was running late. The icy world became too much for many of us. My wings were damaged by the frost, and I fell to the earth. As she hurried across the land, Ostara found me, and felt terrible."

"She laid me where she knew I would be found and cared for. After you lovely people went to bed, she visited me in the moonlight. She said she was sorry, that I would never fly again even if she healed me. So she transformed me into one of her fastest runners as a way to make amends... and here we are!"

"Gracious," said Mama. "You *have* been through a lot. Well, you're welcome to stay here for as long as you need. Why don't you come to the Festival with us? It will do you some good."

"That sounds nice," replied the Hare. "I'd love to come. Thank you."

"Yay!" squealed the Witchlings, giving the Large Lapin a big cuddle.

"Let's gather the baskets," said Mama.

"Here," smiled Rose Witchling. "You can borrow my scarf. It's chilly today."

When they arrived at the Festival, they made their way through the crowd to the barn.

As Mama added their basket to the Treat Hunt table, a sudden gust of wind blew through from outside and threw the barn doors shut with a deafening *BANG!!*

The Hare, startled by the sharp noise, panicked & tried to fly away, forgetting that he no longer could. He smashed into the table & knocked everything onto the floor.

"I'm so very, very sorry!" he cried.

"Nobody was hurt. Accidents happen," said Mama, stroking his fur gently. "Why don't you go outside and calm down while we clean this up."

So the Hare left the barn while everyone did
what they could to mop up the mess. There
were lots of excited questions about the tall
fluffy visitor from the Festival guests, and
even though the Treat Hunt was now
cancelled, everyone was still very happy that
he came.

Just as the last of the crumbs were swept, the
Hare bounced back in with a huge smile on his
face.

"I'm so sorry that I ruined the first Hunt," he
said quickly, "But I think I may have created
something even better. Come see!"

When the Witchlings stepped outside, they couldn't believe what they saw. Eggs! Eggs everywhere! Spotty ones, stripey ones, chequered ones, rainbow ones. All dotted around the Festival grounds.

"Lady Ostara was waiting for me when I came outside," explained the Hare. "She wished to honour my earlier life as a bird, so gave me back the ability to lay eggs, except these eggs are a little… different."

"Different how?" asked Lily Witchling.

"You'll see," he grinned in response.

The happiness amongst the gatherers was wonderful. Everyone was smiling, racing, seeking, searching. The excitement tripled almost instantly when someone discovered that the eggs weren't normal eggs, but were in fact made of chocolate!

"What a delicious surprise!" said Lily Witchling, her face covered in cocoa smears.

As the end of the day drew near, Mama asked the Hare if he still wanted to stay with them for a while.

"That's such a kind offer," he smiled, "But I think I'd like to keep bringing joy to children. I'm going to travel the world."

"Wait, you're leaving?" cried the Witchlings.

"I am sorry," he replied gently. "But I cannot ignore my Calling. But I promise to visit you every Spring Equinox, and leave you a gift."

He gave both girls a big hug, and began to hop away.

"Blessed Ostara!" he shouted.

The
END!

Ostara

Upon my sill
there sits a box
Of earthy soil
and pretty rocks
A gift has lain
for quite a while
Just waiting for
the Sun to smile
With blinking eyes
With stretch & yawn
A new green bud
Of nature, born
So small yet strong
This precious crumb...
The Equinox
Of Spring has come

Did you enjoy this story?

LOOK OUT FOR MORE ADVENTURES IN THE TWO LITTLE WITCHLINGS SERIES!

- **Beltane**
- **Litha**
- **Lammas**
- **Mabon**
- **Samhain**
- **Yule**
- **Imbolc**